UNIT	CHRISTIANITY PART 1	CHRISTIANITY PART 2	BUDDHISM	HINDUISM	ISLAM	JUDAISM	SIKHISM	THEMES
UNIT 1	The birth and death of Jesus	The light of the world	The story of Siddhartha	One God, many faces	Muhammad and the Ka'bah	Moses and the Ten Commandments	The ten Gurus and the history of Sikhism	Beginnings
UNIT 2	Worship at home	Worship in church	Meditation	Hindus at prayer	Talking to Allah	Jews at prayer	Sikh worship	Prayer and worship
UNIT 3	Special places	Holy Communion	A Buddhist shrine	Worship in the mandir	What is in a mosque?	Worship in the synagogue	The gurdwara	Places of worship
UNIT 4	Christmas	Advent	Wesak, the festival of Buddha	Holi	Ramadan, the month of fasting	Celebrating Pesach	Baisakhi celebration	Festivals
UNIT 5	Easter	Lent	Kathina Day, celebrating monasteries	Raksha Bandhan	Celebrating Id-ul-Fitr	Rosh Hashanah and Yom Kippur	Divali	Festivals
UNIT 6	Stories from the Bible	The Bible	The Tripitaka, the holy book of Buddhists	Hindu holy books	Exploring the Qur'an	The Torah, teaching and telling	The Guru Granth Sahib	Holy books
UNIT 7	The Christian family	The Christian family	The Sangha, the family of Buddhism	Hindu family life	Learning the Muslim way	Shabbat Shalom	Sikh family life	Family
UNIT 8	Baptism	Confirmation	Welcome to the family	The first haircut	Welcoming a baby	Bar and Bat Mitzvah	The Amrit ceremony	Rites of passage
UNIT 9	Marriage	Death	Ordination	A Hindu wedding	A Muslim wedding	A Jewish wedding	Sikh funerals	Rites of passage
UNIT 10	Christian art	Christian art	The Buddha in art	The artistic heritage of Hinduism	Calligraphy	Heaven and Earth	Art in Sikhism	Art and inspiration

Introduction

Living Religions is a new R. E. course for the whole primary school, which gives teachers a practical programme of study and clear guidelines for teaching Religious Education. **Living Religions** contains a wide range of flexible classroom activities allowing you to teach, with confidence, the six major world faiths:

 Christianity   **Buddhism**   **Hinduism**

 Islam   **Judaism**   **Sikhism**

Who has developed Living Religions?

The series editor is Chris Richards, Inspector for R. E. at the Northamptonshire Inspection and Advisory Service, whose expertise has ensured that the course has been created by a team of experienced R. E. educators and developed in close consultation with members of all respective faith groups. In addition, extensive trialling and consultation with teacher focus groups has ensured the course matches the requirements of all primary teachers.

Course components for Living Religions

Each of the six religions has a Teacher's Resource Book and a supporting Poster Pack. In the case of Christianity, there are two Teacher's Resource Books and two Poster Packs.

Each **Teacher's Resource Book** includes:

- a concise introduction to the religion and key terminology;
- ten units of work based on key themes;
- a wide range of clearly differentiated activities;
- stories for the teacher to read aloud;
- photocopiable activity sheets for independent work.

Each **Poster Pack** includes:

- ten large, A2–size, full–colour posters (one for each unit of work);
- excellent teacher support on the reverse sides, including background information and ideas for discussion.

Living Religions and your Local Agreed Syllabus and the Scottish Guidelines for Religious and Moral Education 5–14

The series has been developed to meet the requirements of the new generation of agreed syllabuses based on the model syllabus guidelines issued by SCAA in 1994.

Living Religions also meets the needs of the first two attainment outcomes in the 5–14 Guidelines relating to Christianity and Other World Religions.

It ensures systematic coverage which gives integrity to the study of each religion. At the same time, a similar series of themes is explored across religions which make it easy to follow a thematic syllabus (see page 1).

Flexibility in the curriculum

Living Religions has been designed to reflect current primary practice by linking with other subjects and allowing for topic-based teaching. It links with other areas of the curriculum not only through content, but also through the development of speaking and listening skills, expansion of vocabulary, inculcation of empathy and understanding, and personal and social skills.

Differentiation in Living Religions

The activities in the Teacher's Resource Books are based on three levels of ability:

- **Core** activities are for children who are broadly of average ability;
- **Extension** activities are for children of higher than average ability or slightly older children;
- **A more basic approach** offers activities suitable for children of lower than average ability or slightly younger children.

Assessment in Living Religions

Many of the activities in **Living Religions** give children a chance to show what they have learned and understood. Their response to these activities can be assessed. The assessment opportunity is shown by the symbol

Additional materials for Christianity

In recognition of the fact that many schools will devote a larger proportion of time to teaching it, two Teacher's Resource Books are provided for Christianity:

Christianity Part 1 Teacher's Resource Book and Poster Pack is suitable for ages 4 to 7;

Christianity Part 2 Teacher's Resource Book and Poster Pack is suitable for ages 7 to 11.

Note: At the end of this Teacher's Resource Book you will find a list of books about Judaism. We do not recommend these books, but the list includes some books available at the time of writing, should you require extra resources.

Judaism – Some key facts

Jews are very proud of their history, which they can trace back to ancient times to the Patriarch, Abraham, known as the father of the Hebrews. Abraham believed in one God, and made a covenant or agreement that if Abraham obeyed God, then in return God would make his descendants more numerous than the stars. The sign of that covenant is circumcision.

Later, when God revealed the commandments to Moses on Mount Sinai, the Israelites as a people entered into this covenant, promising that they would serve God by keeping all the commandments, or mitzvot. There are 613 in all, the most famous being the Ten Commandments.

The commandments affect all aspects of Jewish life including what they may and may not eat, and therefore make Jewish people distinctive. Jews are sometimes known as 'am-sefer', 'the people of the book', and treat their scriptures with great respect. The scriptures consist of three parts:

1   the Torah, the Five Books of Moses, is the most sacred since it contains the revelations of God to Moses on Mount Sinai;

2   the Nevi'im, the Books of the Prophets, e.g. Joshua, Jeremiah;

3   the Ketuvim, Holy Writings, e.g. Psalms and Proverbs.

The initials T, N, K are used in the word 'Tenakh'. This is the name given by Jews to their scriptures.

The most important day of the week for Jews is Shabbat, lasting from just before sunset on Friday evening to Saturday evening, when stars appear in the sky. Shabbat will be celebrated with special prayers and rituals in the home and synagogue. The synagogue is the place of worship, which is also a place where Jews meet together as a community. No work is permitted on Shabbat.

Judaism has many festivals, including:

The Days of Awe. These include the festival of Rosh Hashanah (New Year), followed ten days later by Yom Kippur (the Day of Atonement), the most solemn day of the Jewish Year.

The most important pilgrim festival, Pesach (Passover) which remembers the time of slavery in Egypt and God's deliverance of the Israelites.

Hanukkah, a festival celebrating deliverance and associated with light.

Sukkot, the Feast of the Tabernacles, which is associated with harvest.

Purim, based on the story of Esther.

Jewish people have a sense of belonging. They belong first to God, since they believe He has chosen them to serve him through the covenants. The daily routine of keeping the commandments required of them is a constant reminder of this special relationship and responsibility.

Jews have a sense of belonging to each other as a world-wide family with its roots in the ancient past. Jews also share the same hope for the future, that one day the Mashiach (or Messiah) will come and bring peace to the world.

Glossary

Aron Hakodesh *(A-ron Hakkodaish)*	holy Ark. The focal point of the synagogue, containing **Torah** scrolls
Bar Mitzvah	son of commandment. A boy's coming of age at 13 years old, usually marked by a synagogue ceremony and family celebration
Bat Mitzvah	daughter of the commandments. A girl's coming of age at 12 years old
Bimah *(Bimma)*	a dais or raised platform primarily for reading the **Torah** in the synagogue
Hagadah	telling. A book used at Seder
Kippah	head covering worn during prayers, **Torah** study, etc. Some followers wear it constantly
Kosher	fit; proper. Foods permitted by Jewish dietary laws
Menorah	seven-branched candelabrum which was lit daily in the Temple
Mitsvah	(plural Mitsvot) commandment. The **Torah** contains 613 Mitsvot. Commonly used to describe good deeds
Ner Tamid *(Nair Tammid)*	eternal light. The perpetual light above the **Aron Hakodesh**
Sefer Torah *(Sayfer To-rah)*	**Torah** scroll. The five books of Moses handwritten on parchment and rolled to form a scroll
Shabbat	day of spiritual renewal and rest commencing at sunset on Friday, terminating at nightfall on Saturday
Shema	major Jewish prayer affirming belief in one God. The Shema is found in the **Torah**
Tallit	prayer shawl. Four-cornered garment with fringes
Tefillin	small leather boxes containing passages from the **Torah**. Tefillin are strapped on the forehead and arm for morning prayers on weekdays
Torah	law; teaching. The Five Books of Moses
Yad	hand-held pointer used in reading the **Sefer Torah**

pronunciations

# UNIT 1
Moses and the Ten Commandments

AIMS

1 The children should hear the story of Moses receiving the Law on Mount Sinai, be able to recall the main events and identify some of the commandments.

2 The children should grow in understanding about the reasons for self-discipline and the importance to Jews of obedience to the word of God.

3 The children should reflect on their own rules and the importance to them of keeping promises.

PREPARATION

For these activities you will need:

- poster 1;
- copies of Activity sheet 1 (page 9);
- several strips of paper with the Ten Commandments;
- an outline picture of a mountain.

Core activities

1 Doing the right thing
(15 mins)

Ask the children what picture comes into their minds when they think of the word 'law'. (Encourage them to identify rules, e.g. do and don't; police; courts.) Ask the children:

- is there a difference between 'law' and 'rule'?

(The children will probably give you examples of specific laws or rules. Look for answers which tend towards the implication that laws may apply to a whole society, whereas rules may have less force and apply to smaller groups of people.)

Brainstorm answers to the question, 'Why do we obey rules?' Collect answers on the board.

(Encourage ideas such as: 'to help everybody'; 'to make an orderly community'; 'because it is sensible'.)

2 The Ten Commandments
(30 mins)

Show the children poster 1, and use the questions and guidance on the reverse to draw out information and meaning from the picture.

Organise the children into groups of about four. Give out strips of paper which have the Ten Commandments written on them (each group should have a complete set). These can be found in Exodus 20. Use a children's Bible to ensure that the language is age-appropriate, or take the commandments from the story that comes with this unit.

Ask each group to consider the laws and agree on an order of importance. They should place the strips in this order on the table. Discuss the results as a class. Is there any common pattern? E.g. does 'Do not kill' come first?

Compare the order of importance the children give with the order in Exodus. It is likely that the children will have put civil laws first, whereas Exodus places the religious laws first. This emphasises the religious nature of the laws for Jews.

3 The story of Moses and the covenant
(30 mins)

Read the story of Moses on page 10. Use the guidance and questions as the basis of a class discussion to draw meaning from the story.

Ensure that the idea is understood that groups/societies/civilisations begin with some kind of common set of rules, laws, beliefs. The Ten Commandments is a good example of this.

4 Rules for living
(45 mins)

Use Activity sheet 1 (page 9) for this activity.

Ask the children to think of five laws which (if everybody obeyed them) would make the world a better place. Ask the children to write these under the title 'Laws to live by' on the activity sheet.

Organise the children into groups, with no more than four in each group. Each group will have up to 20 laws between them. Set the children the task:

- as a group, agree which five laws from all of those you have are the most important.

- Write your agreement on another copy of the activity sheet.

You can look at the finished lists as a class. Each group can explain why they chose their laws, explaining how the keeping of them by everyone will make the world, or just the community, better.

You can make a summary, on sugar paper, for display purposes – to show the top ten laws chosen by the class.

The Ten Commandments

EXTENSION

This extension activity is concerned with making agreements. Discuss with the children what agreement they would like to make as a class (including the teacher) for the following week. The agreement can be very simple, e.g. making sure that everything is put away, or not saying anything unkind. The promise can be written in the form of a charter, e.g.

Teacher: I promise . . .

Class: We promise . . .

Everybody can sign it to show that they agree and have promised. The promise can be displayed for a week. (It can be agreed that the word 'sorry' should be used if anyone breaks the promise!)

A more basic approach

The suggestions on this page will help you adapt the Core teaching and learning activities, making them suitable for younger children or those at an earlier stage of development.

1 Doing the right thing

To help the children to start thinking about rules and laws, give them a number of cards, some of which have rules written on them and some of which have laws. Laws would be, e.g.,

> Drive on the left-hand side of the road.
> Only people over 18 can go into pubs.

Rules would be, e.g.,

> Don't run in the corridors.
> Come to school at 9.00 a.m. every day.

Ask the children to organise these into two lists, and then add their own to each list.

2 The Ten Commandments

This Core activity is suitable for all children. Some children may need to discuss the meaning of each commandment with you, to ensure that they understand.

When the children have agreed on an order of importance for the commandments, do not compare these with the biblical order until after you have looked at the story of Moses in the next activity.

3 The story of Moses and the covenant

When you have read and talked about the story; you can ask the children to draw an outline of Mount Sinai (or provide one for them). Ask the children to choose one of the commandments which God gave the Jewish people/Israelites. The children should decide how to illustrate the commandment. The children should then write and draw a picture of the commandment within the outline of the mountain. They can add details, such as clouds and lightning, to show that something special is happening.

Give children the biblical list of the commandments. Remind the children of the order of importance they put the Ten Commandments into in the last activity, and compare the two lists.

4 Rules for living

This activity is suitable for all children. Some children may need help, from the teacher or classroom assistant, to write down their ideas. This help with the writing will give them an opportunity to talk about their ideas, so that they are more confident in presenting their contribution to the whole class.

All children can contribute to making the class agreement.

ACTIVITY SHEET 1

Laws to live by

Write five laws which you think would make the world better.

1 _____

_____

2 _____

_____

3 _____

_____

4 _____

_____

5 _____

_____

Introducing the story

Jewish people trace their history back to one man – Abraham, originally called Abram, who lived nearly four thousand years ago in the country we now call Iraq. The importance of Abraham to Jews is that he was the first person to propose that there is only one God (monotheism) rather than many Gods (polytheism).

The relationship between the people of Abraham and God is the substance of the history of Jews as told in the Bible. The story of Moses is critical to this history, because it was an important time when the relationship between Jews and their God was encapsulated in a covenant, an agreement made. The story tells of the making of the covenant.

Talking about the story

Ask the children to recall the main points of the story in the following way.

- Why was Mount Sinai a special place for Moses?
  (It is where he first saw God.)

- What was the agreement (or covenant) made between the people of Israel and God?
  (God will look after the Hebrews; the Hebrews will worship God.)

- What were the rules which the Hebrews agreed to keep?
  (the Ten Commandments)

Talk to the children about promises.

- Can you think of times when you have made a promise or when someone has made a promise to you?

- Is it easy or difficult to keep a promise?
  (Encourage the children to recognise that this would depend on the promise.)

- Why might people make promises?
  (E.g. they might make a promise to behave better – the promise might help them to do this. Children may talk about promises in terms of keeping secrets for friends/others – you can extend this discussion to talk about good and bad promises in this context, and the importance of considering promises made, and using good judgment.)

- How easy do you think it would be to keep the Ten Commandments?

The story of Moses and the covenant

During the time of Moses, many Hebrew people lived in Egypt. At fir[s] they had lived peacefully beside the Egyptians. But a new King came to power; he was a very cruel man an[d] made them all into slaves. He order[ed] that baby boys born to them shoul[d] be murdered.

This Pharaoh had a kind daughter who found a baby boy hidden in th[e] bulrushes beside the river Nile. She adopted him and brought him up [as] an Egyptian prince, calling him Moses.

When he had grown up, Moses wen[t] to another country where he marrie[d] and settled down, working as a shepherd for his father-in-law. One day he followed the sheep far into t[he] desert, to Mount Sinai. There he saw [a] marvellous vision of a bush which was ablaze with fire, and yet not destroyed by the flames. From out o[f] this burning bush he heard God's voice calling to him:

"Moses! Go back into Egypt, and go [back] back to Pharaoh's palace. Rescue m[y] people, the Hebrews, from slavery. Tell them that I have sent you. Tell them that I shall take them to a lan[d] of their own, a land flowing with m[ilk] and honey!"

Moses did go back to Egypt and afte[r] some time, a lot of difficulty and a [lot] of sadness (but that is another story[)] he led his people into freedom. At first, the Egyptian King's army tried [to] follow them, but God worked more miracles so that the army was destroyed, and the Hebrews safely escaped.

After that, Moses led the Hebrews through a desert wilderness for a ve[ry] long time. Sometimes they ran out [of] food and almost died of starvation, but God sent them sweet manna (o[r] food) from heaven to eat. Later on they could find no water, and at on[e] time it looked as if they might die o[f] thirst, but God told Moses to strike [a] rock with his stick, and at once a ring of fresh water came gushing out for them to ink. However difficult things were, God always ade sure that his people survived.

t the people did not always behave as well as God ped.

ter a long time, Moses led them to the bottom of ount Sinai. Here they stopped and made a camp. oses told them they must wait there and prepare for mething extraordinary, for very soon God himself as going to speak to them!

he people cleaned their camp and washed their othes, getting ready for God. Three days passed. ddenly a great storm seemed to explode out of the ountain, with peals of thunder and flashes of ghtning. The mountain top became lost in swirling ist, and a loud trumpet blast ripped through the y.

he people stood at the foot of Mount nai, gazing up at its peak. Flames shed out of the mist, and the umpet blast grew louder and uder. Moses cried out to God, nd God answered in eafening claps of thunder. hen God called to Moses, lling him to go up alone the very top of the ountain.

here in the swirling ists on top of Mount

Sinai, God gave Moses his special laws, the Ten Commandments. First God spoke them aloud; then he carved them out on two great tablets of stone.

Moses came down the mountain, back to the desert, carrying the stone tablets. He repeated the Ten Commandments to his people, explaining that, if they always obeyed them, they would live together in happiness and peace.

The people listened. They knew that it would not be easy to keep the Ten Commandments, but they made a solemn promise that they would try.

God was very pleased. Before long, He kept his own promise to the Hebrews, and took them into their new country, which was really a wonderful, fertile land 'flowing with milk and honey'.

UNIT 2
Jews at prayer

AIMS

1 The children should recognise and identify the Jewish symbols associated with prayer.

2 The children should be able to give a simple explanation of the meaning of these symbols and the reasons why people use them.

3 The children should grow in understanding about the way in which outer symbols can remind people of important beliefs and ideas.

PREPARATION

For these activities you will need:

● poster 2;

● copies of Activity sheet 2 (page 15);

● examples of Jewish artefacts, particularly Kippah, Tallit and Tefillin, and/or line drawings of these artefacts;

● the words of the Shema, preferably from a children's Bible, found in: Deuteronomy 6:4–9; Exodus 13:1–10; Exodus 13:11–16; Deuteronomy 11:13–21;

● small pieces of card, each with a hole punched in one end like a luggage label;

● lengths (of approx. 20 cm) of coloured wool (one for each child);

● examples of Hebrew lettering from reference books on Judaism.

Core activities

1 Outward signs
(20 mins)

Ask the children to give you examples of how they might know what a person is going to do by the clothes they are wearing. Write examples on the board, under two columns:

Someone wearing:	Might be going to:
football scarf	football match

Draw out from the discussion that clothes can be outward signs which may tell us something about the person and what they do. They may not just be objects in themselves.

You will need to agree with the children that a person's clothing and outward appearance does not necessarily indicate anything about that person.

2 Dressing for prayer
(30 mins)

Show them the poster, and tell the children that this is an example of when outward signs (the things the boy is wearing) tell us something about him and what he is doing.

Use the questions and guidance on the reverse of the poster to explore what is special about the boy and his clothing.

3 Tallit, Tefillin and Kippah
(70 mins)

If you have a Tallit and Kippah, allow these to be handled and examined by the children. If you have Tefillin, do not allow these to be passed around and tried on. Treating the Tefillin with great respect will communicate more effectively the special nature of the objects to Jews.

Spend 20/25 minutes looking at each of the three.

A About the tefillin

Read the opening words of the Shema (Deuteronomy 6:4–9) slowly to the children, allowing time for appreciation and reflection.

Ask the children to think of things which they might want to say to themselves and remember each day, words to keep in their hearts. (Some children may not want to share aloud, and this should be respected.)

Use Activity sheet 2 (page 15) to record the words. Ask the children to fold them and keep them in a special place for a week, and encourage them to read them each day.

B About the Tallit

Remind the children that the Tallit is to remind the Jewish people of the commandments.

Ask the children to think of things, people or ideas that they want to be reminded of during the day, e.g. special people, people who are ill or in need, or a reminder to be kind or helpful.

Give out the pieces of punched card and lengths of wool. Ask children to put their names on the card, thread the wool through the holes, and tie knots in the wool (one for each of their 'reminders').

(The children can keep their 'reminders' in their drawer or box for the week. Use them each day, perhaps as part of class assembly, to remind them of their thoughts.)

C About the Kippah

Remind the children that the Kippah is worn to show respect. Ask the children in what other ways might someone show respect? Make a list of examples such as: use of titles (sir, madam); putting things in special places; wearing special clothes for special occasions; opening doors for special people.

Special clothing – dressing for prayer

EXTENSION

More able children can find the opening verses of the Shema in the Bible using the text references given on the reverse of the poster. Verses may be copied on a small scroll, and children can make a box to keep it in.

Explain to the children that the man on the poster always prays and uses the special clothes in the same way. Where people have certain ways of doing things which are always the same, and in the same order, this is called a routine or ritual. Following a set routine helps people remember what to do and to concentrate on the important things.

Ask children to identify other rituals, e.g. secular rituals – taking the register; assembly; getting ready for bed; religious rituals – other religious services and ceremonies such as weddings.

Ask the children to make a list of all the stages in one of the rituals. They should number the separate stages.

A more basic approach

The suggestions on this page will help you adapt the Core teaching and learning activities, making them suitable for younger children or those at an earlier stage of development.

1 Outward signs

Find pictures, in catalogues/magazines/newspapers, of people dressed for special events. Write the names of the events on card.

Ask the children to match the name of the event to the correct picture.

Talk about the idea that what you wear can sometimes tell a lot about who you are and what you are doing.

Alternatively, you can bring in examples of special clothes and special objects, e.g. a big hat; a special scarf; swimming goggles; a shopping bag; a school bag; a special tie; binoculars.

Ask the children:

● 'If I were wearing/carrying these, where would I be going?'

2 Dressing for prayer

Use the artefacts if at all possible. If not, prepare line drawings of the three sets of artefacts for the children. These can be labelled and/or coloured.

3 Tallit, Tefillin and Kippah

Instead of reading the Shema to the children, you can talk to them about special words, and help them to think of and write their own words on the activity sheet.

Make the card and wool 'reminder' in the same way.

Keep both the reminder and the activity sheet for the children. Give them both back to the children each day for a week, so they can read the activity sheet and try to remember what the wool is supposed to remind them of.

Help the children make a Kippah in the following way:

Give out circles of paper.

If possible, the children should decorate the border with Hebrew letters. Give the children examples, such as

אבגדהוזח

If you cut to just beyond the centre of the circle, you can staple the shape into a small Kippah.

The completed Kippahs can be made into a display.

ACTIVITY SHEET 2   **My special words**

Write your special words on this paper.

Fold the paper up and keep it safe for a week.

Look at it each day.

_____

_____

_____

_____

_____

_____

_____

_____

UNIT 3
Worship in the synagogue

AIMS

1 The children should recognise that Jews worship collectively in the synagogue as well as at home.

2 The children should be able to identify some of the features of a synagogue and explain some of the symbolism of those features.

3 The children should grow in understanding of why people meet together to worship their God.

PREPARATION

For these activities you will need:

● poster 3 (with labels for the important features);

● copies of Activity sheet 3 (page 19) and the supplementary activity sheet (page 52);

● a candle or flame;

● blackcurrant juice and biscuits.

If possible:

● a video showing worship in a synagogue.

Core activities

1 The synagogue
(30 mins)

Introduce the activity by telling the children that you are going to learn about the synagogue, the special place of worship for Jewish people.

Show the children poster 3 and use the questions and guidance on the reverse of the poster to lead a discussion about this special place.

Make cards with the names of all the key features of the synagogue: Aron Hakodesh; bimah; Ten Commandments; rabbi; scrolls; Magen David (star of David); menorah.

Display these cards as each feature is noted. End the activity by pinning the poster on the wall and asking individual children to put the labels in the correct place.

2 In the synagogue
(50 mins)

If possible, have a video which shows a service in a synagogue.

Show the video and talk about the activities which are seen. Pause the video frequently and make a list of the different activities.

Give children a copy of Activity sheet 3 (page 19).

Ask the children to make a leaflet which could be given to visitors as a guide to a synagogue. The activity sheet gives eight headings which would need to be written about. Children need to write the text and add any other features.

Talk about the task, to decide what a visitor would need to know and how the leaflet could be made attractive. If possible, use I.T. to prepare and print the leaflet.

3 Special places and special feelings
(30 mins)

Show the poster again. Remind the

children about the eternal light – the ner tamid. Ask the children what 'eternal' means. Look for answers describing, e.g., something as 'going on forever', 'everlasting', 'infinity'.

Ask how the ner tamid helps Jewish people to think and wonder about God. Encourage the children to identify that the Jews believe their God to be eternal.

Place a candle (or a small lamp) where all the class can see it. Ask the children to look at the flame. When the children are settled and contemplative, ask them to think about something special and important to them.

After a few moments, ask them to think of a place which is special to them because of the way it makes them feel or because of what happens there. Ask them to try to imagine, without talking about it, that they are in their special place. They should think about how that makes them feel.

The supplementary activity sheet on page 52 has a shape of a flame. Give copies to children, asking them to colour the flame, and write words about how they felt when they looked into the flame.

4 Kiddush
(10 mins)

Remind the children that after the service in a synagogue, the congregation gather to drink wine and eat cake.

Say that you are going to end the lesson in the same way, to see what it feels like.

Give children a small drink of blackcurrant juice and a biscuit. Ask them to talk to each other about what they have been doing in the lesson.

After five minutes, ask the children to shake hands, and bring them back together to talk about how they feel. Try to distinguish between their feelings of excitement due to the novelty, and the feelings of sharing resulting from the talking.

The synagogue

EXTENSION

Ask the children to imagine that they are in the synagogue shown on the poster. They can talk about how each thing has meaning and discuss how Jewish people show that it is special, e.g. Torah is read using a yad (Jews would not touch the Torah, to indicate how special the words are). Look at features of the synagogue; special clothes; special actions.

They should use other books and resources to find further information about what they see in the poster.

If possible, arrange a visit to a synagogue.

A more basic approach

The suggestions on this page will help you adapt the Core teaching and learning activities, making them suitable for younger children or those at an earlier stage of development.

1 The synagogue

When discussing the poster, place all the cards with special words on the board beside the poster.

Together, the children can recognise each word, and say where to place it on the poster.

Have posters 1 and 2 on show, to remind the children of their previous learning.

2 In the synagogue

If you have a video of a service in a synagogue, prepare a brief list of actions that can be seen on the video.

Write a description of each action on separate cards, mix them up, and give them to the children.

Stop the video after each episode and ask the children which of the cards describes what they have just seen.

Place the cards in the correct order where children can see them.

To make the visitors' guide, give the children simple line drawings of the objects mentioned on Activity sheet 3 (page 19), and a simple sentence about each one.

The children should match the picture and simple description to the correct heading.

3 Special places and special feelings

After the children have finished looking into the flame, talk with them about the feelings they had and the images they saw.

Write the words down where children can see them.

The children can then select the words that appeal to them most, and write them onto the flame shape.

4 Kiddush

This activity is suitable for all children.

ACTIVITY SHEET 3   **A guide to the synagogue**

Aron Hakodesh

_____

_____

_____

_____

Ner tamid

_____

_____

_____

_____

Bimah

_____

_____

_____

_____

Torah

_____

_____

_____

_____

Rabbi

_____

_____

_____

_____

Ten Commandments

_____

_____

_____

_____

Menorah

_____

_____

_____

_____

Star of David

_____

_____

_____

_____

UNIT 4
Celebrating Pesach

AIMS

1 The children should recognise and know about some of the customs associated with Passover.

2 The children should be able to identify and explain some of the symbols used at the Seder meal.

3 The children should develop their understanding of the ways in which remembering and celebrating can influence life.

PREPARATION

For these activities you will need:

- poster 4;
- copies of Activity sheet 4 (page 23);
- a collection of logos or symbols;
- a Remembrance Day poppy;
- napkins and red liquid.

If possible:

- matzah;
- a video of a Passover celebration;
- other artefacts, e.g. a Seder dish.

Core activities

1 Signs
(15 mins)

Find a number of common symbols or logos which the children will recognise. Road signs and common commercial logos (e.g. McDonalds) are good examples.

Show the symbols to the children, and ask them to identify each one.

Discuss why it is so easy to identify the signs. Talk about how these symbols can signify meaning and information in a simple way.

Finally, show the children a poppy. Ask the children to say what the poppy stands for (Remembrance Day) and why the poppy was chosen as the symbol of this. Other connections should be made between the symbol itself (the poppy) and what is being remembered. Ensure that a link is made between the colour of the poppy and the colour of blood; also identify that the flower can be a symbol of new life.

2 The story of the Exodus
(30 mins)

Read the children the story of the plagues of Egypt and the Passover on page 24.

Use the questions and guidance with the story to help the children draw meaning and information from it.

3 Happy things, sad things
(15 mins)

Explain to the children that the event described in the story on page 24 is very important to Jews. This is why they have a festival to remember it every year. Some of the things they remember about the Exodus are happy, some are very sad.

As part of a class/group discussion, or as an individual activity in which the results are compared, encourage the children to make a list under the following two headings: 'happy things about the Exodus'; 'sad things about the Exodus'.

4 The Passover meal
(30 mins)

Show the children poster 4, which shows a Jewish family at the Seder meal which celebrates the Passover.

Use the questions and guidance on the reverse of the poster to talk about the scene shown. Ensure that the children know what takes place during the meal, and can recognise the symbolism of the foods.

If possible, have some matzah and perhaps other food for Seder for the children to taste. If you can possibly arrange it, have a video of a Passover meal which can be shown to the children.

5 Remembering sadness
(30 mins)

The most solemn and powerful moment during the Seder meal is when the plagues are remembered. The father of the family names each plague in turn. The rest of the family repeat the words, whilst the father dips his finger into a glass of wine and places a drop of the wine onto a napkin. Each drop of wine represents the fact that some of the rejoicing (the wine) is spoilt by the death of the Egyptians.

You can encourage the children to help you to act out this part of the meal: name the plagues and place drops of red liquid onto a napkin, and get the children to repeat your words.

Use Activity sheet 4 (page 23) for this activity. Ask the children to think about things that they, as a class or community, may sometimes feel sad about. Encourage the children to identify general rather than personal sadnesses, e.g. they might identify that they should feel sad about the people who have no home, or who are victims of violence or bullying.

The children can go on to express their thoughts individually, in a word or simple phrase, written in each tear on the activity sheet. When they have finished writing, you can ask the children to shade each tear red (to symbolise suffering). The children can discuss their answers as a class, identifying the many similarities between them.

A Jewish family at the Seder meal

EXTENSION

Look at the things which the children have written in their tears. Ask them to identify those which are the most common, and write them into a class set of tears.

Collect them together to form the basis for a class prayer. Speak and repeat the words in each tear and put drops of red-coloured water onto a napkin, to symbolise suffering (as in the seder meal).

A more basic approach

The suggestions on this page will help you adapt the Core teaching and learning activities, making them suitable for younger children or those at an earlier stage of development.

1 Signs

Make some logos into flashcards. Show them until the children can recognise the symbols.

Give the children some magazines. Let them find other examples of symbols and logos.

2 The story of the Exodus

The story on page 24, and the questions and guidance with it, are suitable for all children. You can follow up the story and discussion by making large cards to show the name of each plague.

Divide the class into groups, and give each group one or more of the cards. Encourage the groups to think about how they might act out their plague, e.g. by scratching (the plague of lice); some children can be flies/frogs and others the people plagued by them; or the children may simply act out people crying. Give the children a few minutes to think about, practise and agree, in their groups, how they will do this. It is important for the children to understand and express that the plagues, as told of in the story, did involve real suffering.

Tell the story again and ask each group to hold up their cards at the appropriate point in the story.

After the plague is named, the group can demonstrate the effect of the plague on the people of Egypt.

3 Happy things, sad things

Give out sets of cards or papers with the following prepared sentences (one on each card/paper):

> We were slaves in Egypt. We were set free. The people of Egypt suffered from plagues. Our God helped us. The oldest son died. We escaped from Egypt. We had a great leader called Moses. The Pharaoh would not let us go.

Through discussion, ask the children to help you to sort these into happy and sad lists.

It is important to reiterate and ensure that the children understand that the plagues themselves make Jewish people feel sad for all the suffering caused.

4 The Passover meal

Use the information given on the reverse of the poster to help you to prepare a list of the activities which are part of a Seder meal. Use it to show the children what happens during the meal.

5 Remembering sadness

Use the large cards made in Activity 2 to remind the children about the plagues.

Say the name of each plague aloud, show the children the word, and put drops of red-coloured water onto a napkin as you speak. Explain to the children that this is to indicate that each plague caused suffering (which Jewish people remember in this way at Passover).

After you have done this, talk to the children about the kinds of feeling that this activity evoked in them. Allow them to consider their response thoughtfully, in silence and for a few moments, before they begin talking.

Tears of sadness

What things make us sad?

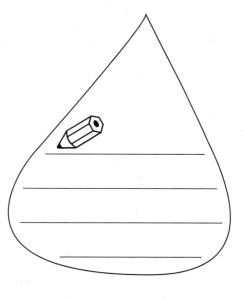

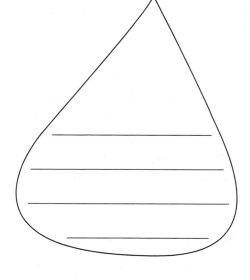

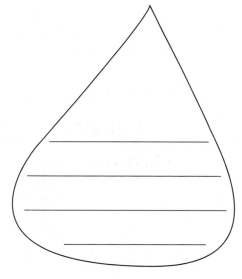

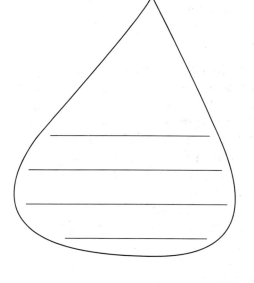

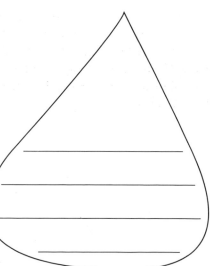

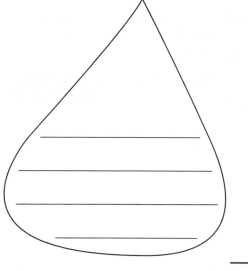

Introducing the story

According to the Bible, Joseph, his brothers and his father, Jacob, settled in Egypt during a time of famine. For many years after that time, the Hebrews had lived in peace in the land of Egypt. Some time later, however, a new King came to the throne and blamed all the country's ills on the presence of the Hebrews. This resulted in the many thousands of Hebrews in Egypt being enslaved, forced to do heavy labouring work. Moses was called by God to save the Hebrews and lead them out of slavery. (This is a complex story for children to understand, particulary in modern terms, so do not be afraid to make this point to the children.)

Talking about the story

- What reason did Pharaoh give for not letting the people go free?
  (He said that there would be nobody to do the work of the slaves.)

- How do you think Moses might have felt when he stood in front of this most powerful King?
  (frightened, overawed)

- How do you think Moses had the courage to keep on asking Pharaoh when he kept on refusing?
  (Moses thought that God had told him what to say and do.)

- What were the ten plagues named in this story?
  (frogs; river Nile turned into blood; lice; flies; plague on the cattle; boils; hail; locusts; darkness; death of the firstborn sons)

- Apart from the last plague, which one would you find the most difficult to live through?

- Why did the Egyptian children die but not the Hebrew children?
  (According to the Bible they were protected by the blood on the doorposts.)

- Why was this the last straw for Pharaoh?
  (His own son died.)

The story of the Exodus

Many years ago, Egypt was ruled by a powerful and cruel King, called Pharaoh. In those days, a King was thought of as being almost like a God. He would have been very powerful, and the people of his land would have had very good reason to fear him.

But there were many people in Pharaoh's land who didn't really worry about Pharaoh. They lived their lives in peace, freely going about their business and watching their children happily playing in the beautiful, sun-soaked and plentiful land of Egypt.

However, Pharaoh did not allow everyone in his land to live freely and in peace. The Hebrews had been made slaves by another Egyptian King, many years before. This meant that they, and their children had to work hard all day in the fields, in the merciless heat. They had to do as they were told and were hardly even treated like people. If they rebelled and stood up for themselves, or even if they just weren't strong enough to do the back-breaking labour which Pharaoh forced them to do, then they would be brutally beaten.

But there was one Hebrew in Egypt at that time, who was not a slave. This man's name was Moses. Moses went into the desert and prayed to God. He asked him to help the Hebrews, his people.

God heard Moses and told him to go to Pharaoh and ask him to let his people go free.

And so a few days later, still hot and dusty from the desert, Moses found himself approaching the King's great throne room. And this is where our story begins.

Moses went up to the tall, heavy doors, which were made of gold and covered with jewels and splendid engravings and, trembling with fear, pulled the huge doors open and walked up the long carpet to Pharaoh's throne.

"Pharaoh," he said, "let the Hebrews, my people, go free!"

Pharaoh turned to Moses with a strange smile. He looked Moses up and down for some moments. Then Pharaoh spoke, slowly and with contempt in his voice: "Why should I?" he asked Moses. His words seemed to hover in the air for a while, and then he smiled and continued, talking in the same even tones: "Who will do all the work, if not my slaves, the Hebrews?"

Moses felt almost overcome by his anger but when he replied to the King, it was with a calm and confident voice.

"I'll say it again – let my people go! If you do not do as I ask you, God will turn the great river Nile into blood as both a warning and a punishment."

"So be it," said Pharaoh, after a pause. "Let us see the power of this God of the Hebrews."

Moses walked away from the Pharaoh quickly, whilst he was still in control of his emotions. He spent the whole of that night pacing his room anxiously. The next day, just as the sun rose, Moses woke up to a terrible screaming and chattering from below his window. During the night, the great river Nile had turned blood red. The fish had all died, and nobody had been able to drink or water their fields. The people of Egypt were amazed by the river. "A river that turns into *blood*!" they said to one another, and they huddled together in their homes, afraid.

Moses went back to Pharaoh, who had already heard of the strange happening. Pharaoh was pacing up and down in front of his throne, but he looked up when Moses entered his room. Pharaoh stared at Moses as he spoke.

"I warned you that the river would turn into blood," said Moses, "and it has happened. Now will you let my people go?"

"No!" Pharaoh spoke in a powerful tone, in spite of his unease. "This has obviously been some kind of trick!" he said sharply. "Get out!"

Moses stayed long enough to deliver another warning to the King. "Plagues will come to Egypt, Pharaoh. They will come one after another. And they will keep on coming until you let my people go free."

Pharaoh watched Moses as he walked slowly away, and out through the splendid doors. He watched the doors close behind Moses and he sat on, without moving, for some time.

That night, Egypt was overrun by millions and millions of frogs. There were frogs everywhere – they got into the houses, people found them under the covers when they got into their beds, they discovered them in their slippers when they got up in the morning. They found frogs in their breakfast as they started to eat. There were frogs in their pockets and frogs everywhere they tried to sleep.

Pharaoh was furious. "Never!" he could be heard shouting, from outside the palace, his words ringing in the heads of people going about their business in the streets below: "I WILL NEVER GIVE IN!"

The next day, the people of Egypt were plagued with biting, crawling lice which nearly drove them mad with itching.

After the frogs and the lice, there was a plague of flies, and a plague on the cattle, which all died, leaving their owners worrying about where the milk would now come from. This was followed by a plague of boils, a plague of hail, a plague of locusts and, one day, a plague of darkness, which made people think that the light of the sun would never come back.

After each plague, Moses returned to Pharaoh to ask him to let his people go free. Each time, Pharaoh was convulsed with fury and sent him packing. And the plagues kept on coming.

Then Moses gathered together all of the Hebrews, and he spoke to the crowd: "Tonight, the last and most terrible plague will pass over Egypt and will kill the firstborn son in every family."

Every mother and father gathered moaned in terror.

Then Moses said, "Don't be afraid. Follow my instructions carefully and your children will not be harmed: tonight you must kill a lamb and wipe its blood across your doorpost. Then pack up your things and make some bread for the journey. Tomorrow, we will be free!"

That night, so the story goes, the Angel of Death flew over Egypt and the oldest son in each house died. This did not happen in the Hebrew homes because the Angel saw the sign of lamb's blood on the doorposts and did not enter.

Early in the morning, as the Hebrews silently made their escape out of Egypt, they could hear in the distance a great cry going up all over the land, a cry of sadness and of mourning, as the Egyptians discovered that they had lost their sons. The Hebrews covered their faces and wept for some moments when they heard these sounds, but they had to move on quickly to save their families and travel on towards freedom.

Back in Egypt, the Pharaoh had covered his head and was crying over the death of his oldest son. "Let them go!" he groaned. "Let them go, so that there will be no more plagues sent to the land of Egypt."

 # UNIT 5

Rosh Hashanah and Yom Kippur

AIMS

1 The children should know about the different customs and traditions with which Jews mark the New Year.

2 The children should develop their understanding of what it means to be sorry and to forgive.

3 The children should be able to identify, and explain the meaning of, the symbols used in this festival, e.g. shofar, apple dipped in honey, and fasting.

PREPARATION

For these activities you will need:

- poster 5;
- copies of Activity sheet 5 (page 29) and supplementary activity sheet (page 53);
- material to make cards.

If possible:

- a shofar, and a video or recording of the sound of a shofar;
- apple slices and honey;
- materials for making birthday cards (page 27);
- birthday cards.

Core activities

1 Being sorry and starting again
(30 mins)

Collect some examples of people doing wrong, perhaps from the newspapers, or perhaps from school. Talk about what might happen to people who do wrong.

Introduce the idea that people can be, or are, sorry for things they do wrong. Ask the children to talk about when they have been sorry, and how they have shown they were sorry, e.g. feeling sad about what has happened, telling somebody about it, apologising and trying to make it better.

2 How Jews say sorry
(15 mins)

Introduce the idea that people sometimes do wrong things and want to find a way to say sorry.

Show the children poster 5. Use the questions on the reverse to draw out information about how Jews say sorry for wrongdoing and ask for forgiveness.

If possible, show the children a real shofar, blow it if you can, and let the children try to produce a note. As an alternative, show a video or listen to a recording of a shofar being blown.

3 Writing a 'sorry' poem
(30 mins)

Ask the children to think quietly for a few minutes about things which make them feel sad. These can be personal things, or more general things about the world or their environment. Play some quiet music whilst this is happening, or light a candle, to help the children to focus and to create a thoughtful atmosphere.

The children can use Activity sheet 5 (page 29) to record the ideas that they generate.

Use these words to brainstorm a class 'sorry' poem, with children contributing about two words each to complete the line: 'We are sorry for . . . (angry actions, hurtful words)'.

4 Happy birthday, world!
(30 mins)

Remind the children that Rosh Hashanah is a time when Jewish people celebrate the birthday of the world. Ask the children: what do we do on birthdays? (We celebrate; we send cards; we give presents.) Tell the children that they are going to make a birthday card to celebrate the birthday of the world. The poster shows examples of Jewish New Year cards.

The children should plan the words and images that they would wish to include on their card. If possible, they can look at some commercially produced birthday cards as a starting point, to both stimulate discussion and help to give them ideas. The children can start by discussing why/whether the images and words on the cards evoke what is required, and go on to brainstorm new ideas for: images (e.g. scenes of togetherness/scenes which inspire); words (e.g. sending love/expressing hope for the future).

Provide stiff paper or card for the finished cards, and make them into a display.

5 New beginnings
(15 mins)

Remind the children about the tradition of making New Year resolutions. Ask the children about any they have made, and whether they were able to keep them. Invite the children to make a new resolution, and write it out on a slip of paper.

Save these resolutions in a 'time capsule'. Hide the time capsule away, to be brought out at an agreed time, later in the term, to see whether anyone has managed to keep their resolution.

You can provide slices of apple dipped in honey and ask the children to share them as they wish each other a sweet and good week ahead.

Jewish symbols – a shofar; apple dipped in honey;

EXTENSION

Use the activity idea on the top part of the supplementary activity sheet on page 53 and ask the children to find the meanings of the words given.

Ask the children to make and complete the chart on the bottom part of the supplementary activity sheet. This will help the children to think about what kind of resolutions they might make, the things which will make them easy to keep, and the things which make them difficult to keep.

A more basic approach

The suggestions on this page will help you adapt the Core teaching and learning activities, making them suitable for younger children or those at an earlier stage of development.

1 Being sorry and starting again

Prepare a small number of example situations in which a person has done something wrong, e.g. treading on somebody's toe; telling a lie; taking a biscuit; hurting somebody's feelings.

Ask the children to think about how they would say sorry in each of these situations.

You can ask the children to role-play certain situations.

The children can be asked to supply two endings: one which helps to put things right and one which makes things worse.

2 How Jews say sorry

After you have used the reverse of poster 5, return to the situations that the children talked about and role-played in the last activity.

Ask the children to think of the words which were used to put things right; write them out. Use a small bell in place of the shofar. After every ring of the bell, speak the 'sorry' words you have prepared. You can ask individuals to do this, or the class in unison.

3 Writing a 'sorry' poem

The children can write individual poems, starting with 'I am sorry for . . .'. In this case, they may need extra help with writing their words.

If you decide to create the poem as a class, you can give the children one or two words describing something to be sorry for, e.g. 'selfish'; 'silly'; 'nasty'; 'angry words/ actions'. Ask the children to think of as many more of these words as they can. Display all of the words and use them to create a class poem, starting each line with 'I am sorry for'/'I am sorry when'/'I am sorry because'. You can ask the children to choose two words each from the list. They should choose their words e.g. because they begin with the same letter; because the words mean something similar; or because they go together in some other way.

4 Happy birthday, world!

Collect some pictures of babies from catalogues. Use them to decorate the birthday cards which celebrate the creation of human beings.

Write out some suitable greetings which the children can select from and copy.

5 New beginnings

This activity is suitable for all children. You can help the children to think of a resolution by giving them some examples: 'always leave my desk tidy'; 'put my coat on the peg'; 'say please and thank you'. Ensure that all the resolutions are achievable!

Write the words for the children, so that they can copy them onto their paper.

Refer to them frequently, so that the children do not forget them or lose interest.

ACTIVITY SHEET 5   I am sorry for . . .

Write the words.

I am sorry for _____

_____

_____

_____

I am sorry that _____

_____

_____

_____

I am sorry when _____

_____

_____

_____

I am sorry because _____

_____

_____

_____

UNIT 6
The Torah, teaching and telling

AIMS

1 The children should be able to recognise the Torah and explain key features of it and the fact that it is read in public services.

2 The children should develop their understanding of, and respect for, the special nature of the Torah to Jewish people.

3 The children should encounter some of the writings included in the Torah.

PREPARATION

For these activities you will need:

● poster 6;

● copies of Activity sheet 6 (page 33).

If possible:

● Bibles;

● quills and ink;

● a model of a Torah scroll;

● a video/tape recording of reading from a scroll.

Core activities

1 Special books
(15 mins)

If you have already talked about 'special books' with the children, this can usefully be treated as a revision exercise. Refer the children to your previous discussion about special books and show them an example of a special book as a starting point.

Ask the children to remember

What makes a book special?
(It contains important stories, teachings, information.)

How are special books treated?
(with respect; with special rituals and ceremonies; they are written carefully; they are protected)

2 The Torah, the special book of Jews
(15 mins)

Show poster 6, and use the questions and guidance on the reverse of the poster to draw information and meaning from the picture.

Remind the children of what you talked about in Activity 1 and ask them to identify the things on the poster which show that the book is special.

Use the information on the reverse of the poster to help you explain to the children how the scrolls are covered and decorated when not in use.

If you have a model Torah, or a video of a Torah being read, you can use it to demonstrate the respect given to special and holy books.

3 Contents of the Torah
(20 mins)

Remind the children about the sort of things that the Torah includes, and find examples in the Bible:

Laws (Deuteronomy 5:17–21. Part of a version of the Ten Commandments.)

History (Exodus 12:31–36. The flight of the Hebrews from Egypt.)

Stories (Genesis 37:3–4; 23–29. Joseph and the coat of many colours.)

(Genesis 2. The story of Adam and Eve.)

Give the children copies of Activity sheet 6 (page 33).

Talk to the children about how some stories are intended to report events and how others may seem to exaggerate in order to convey a certain teaching point/to encourage us to 'dig out' their meaning. Ask the children to try to identify which of the stories are meant to be true accounts and which seem exaggerated (i.e. if stories intended to teach us something).
It is important to note that some people would not regard these as stories but would see them as being true in a literal sense.

4 Making a scroll
(40 mins)

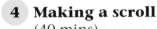

Give each child a few lines from an English translation of one of the books of the Torah.

Ask the children to copy the words exactly, in their best handwriting. If possible, and if the children have the dexterity to handle them, you can use real quills and ink. Afterwards, you can talk to the children about the difficulties in handling these tools, and use the information given on the reverse of poster 6 to talk about how the scribe carries out the task of writing the Torah on the scrolls. Emphasise how the difficulty in creating the scroll shows how important it is to Jewish people.

Take all the writings and stick them together to produce a class scroll on wooden rollers. Use strong card to make a yad.

5 The story of Abraham
(30 mins)

Read the children the story of Abraham on page 34. Use the questions and guidance provided with the story to help the children to draw meaning from it.

Special books – the Torah

EXTENSION

You can use Activity sheet 6 (page 33) to extend Activity 3 by asking children to reference and read the stories.

Extend Activity 4 by placing the class scroll you have made on a table. Let each person come up to the desk and read the section they have written, pointing at each word with the yad you made in Activity 4.

Find some examples of Hebrew script. Ask the children to copy some of the letters, again using the quills and ink if you have them. Ask the children to decorate the class scroll with Hebrew characters.

A more basic approach

The suggestions on this page will help you adapt the Core teaching and learning activities, making them suitable for younger children or those at an earlier stage of development.

1 Special books

Show the children an example of a 'special book' – a book which is special for different (religious/secular) reasons, e.g. a holy book – special to members of that faith; a class register – special to the teacher and members of that class; a book that is special to an individual for personal reasons.

Demonstrate how you would treat a book to show that it is particularly special, e.g. treating it with care; reading it at certain time, and so on. Encourage the children to talk about and demonstrate examples of how they might show that a book is special.

2 The Torah, the special book of Jews

Ensure that the children can recognise the word 'Torah' and what it means, and know what a scroll is. Give the children paper, and let them design a special cover for a scroll, or another special book that you have talked about.

The picture on the poster, and any other references, will help them to select images for the cover of the scroll.

If the children are making a cover for another book, they should talk about and plan the images they will use. First of all, choose the book and then think about how to convey: what the book is about (e.g. key images); that the book is special (e.g. decoration).

3 Contents of the Torah

The activity is suitable for all children, but you may wish to select, from the references given in the Core activities, those stories which are the most appropriate for the level of your class. Ensure that the reading of the different stories from the Torah is taken from a children's Bible so that they can understand the language.

4 Making a scroll

Make sure that the children are given only simple and very short sections of the text to copy onto their contribution to the scroll. If necessary, write their text for them.

If it is appropriate for the children to read aloud to the class, make sure that you give them plenty of practice at reading their section, so that they feel comfortable with reading it.

Where children are unable to write/copy the text, even with guidance, you can find examples of Hebrew writing and allow them to contribute to the class scroll by tracing these to decorate it.

5 The story of Abraham

This activity is suitable for all children. If possible, find a map to show the places mentioned in the story.

ACTIVITY SHEET 6   Contents of the Torah

1 Laws
(Deuteronomy 5:17–21)
There are different versions of the Ten Commandments.
The commandments may be written slightly differently in
each version, but their meaning is always the same.

2 History
(Exodus 12:31–36)
This tells of the escape of the Hebrews from Egypt.

3 Stories
(Genesis 37:3–4; 23–29)
This tells the story of Joseph and his coat of many
colours.
(Genesis 2)
This tells the story of Adam and Eve.

Introducing the story

Abraham is one of the early Patriarchs of the Jewish people. The Torah includes stories about several early Jewish leaders, their encounters with God, and the teachings. These stories chart the history of the covenant (agreement/promise) which was developed between the Jews and God. The stories also explore the nature of God for Jews, and show the development of beliefs and attitudes about God.

After you have read the story, try to get the children to recognise that the important point about the story is what it teaches Jewish people about their God.

Talking about the story

- Why was Haran a good place to live?
  (It was rich and beautiful.)

- What was the land around Haran like?
  (a desert)

- Whose voice did Abraham believe he had heard?
  (God's voice)

- Can you imagine how Abraham felt when he listened to what this voice was saying to him?
  (frightened; tired)

- Why did he not want to do what the voice was telling him?
  (He was happy where he was.)

- Why do you think he obeyed in the end, even though it meant overcoming so many difficulties?
  (He believed in the God who was telling him to move.)

- What was God's promise to Abraham?
  (He would be the father of a great people.)

The story of Abraham

Long ago, in the biblical lands, an old man called Abram heard God speak to him.

"Abram!" said God, "It is time for you to leave home. You must say goodbye to the country of Haran where you have lived for a long time. You must say goodbye to your relations and friends. Take Sarai, your wife, and take all of your servants. Pack up everything that belongs to you and be ready to travel."

Deep inside him, Abram knew the voice to be that of his God. Abram loved the beautiful land of Haran, which was a rich and plentiful area in the middle of the desert. He had no desire to leave behind his home and loved ones. Also, he was an old man at this time and he felt too tired for such an adventure. However, he did exactly as God told him.

When everything was ready, he led Sarai and all of their servants out of Haran. It was a very long journey, and they had to stop to camp at many place along the way.

Abram prayed to God. "Where are we going, Lord?" he asked.

God replied, "To the land of Canaan".

"But . . . why?" Abram wondered.

God said, "Listen Abram, I am going to make you a promise. I shall give you many great grandchildren, and they in turn will have many more children. One day, these descendants of yours will become a great nation. They will remember your name forever!"

Abram was amazed. He built an altar and cried out his thanks and praise to God. Then he travelled on, until at last he arrived safely in Canaan.

God said, "Look around you, Abram. All the land you can see in every direction is for you. It shall pass on to your descendants. This is my promise."

Abram thanked God again. But still he was puzzled. How could he possibly have all of these great grandchildren? He and Sarai were both very old, and they had never had even one baby. It was much too late to start a family now!

God said, "Abram, there will be more children in you family than there are stars in the sky! They will be strong and all this land will be theirs forever".

Abram told Sarai all about it. "Well," she said sadly, "I'm much too old to have a child now. If this is going to come true, you had better find another wife, someone who is still young enough to have babies".

She told Abram to marry Hagar, her servant. He did, and Hagar had a son called Ishmael. Perhaps he would give Abram all the descendants that God had promised!

Time went on and Abram had another vision. This time, God told him, "You are going to be the father of many nations. So you must change your name to 'Abraham', which means, 'The father of countless people'."

Abraham, as he now was, listened carefully. God went on, "Sarai's name must change too. From now on, she shall be called 'Sarah', which means 'Princess'. For I shall bless her with the greatest of treasures: I shall give her a son".

Abraham was more astonished than ever. "But that's impossible!" he cried. "I am almost 100 and Sarah is 90. How can we have a baby together, at our age?"

God said, "Nothing is impossible for me."

Abraham told all his household about the extraordinary things that God had told him. He said they must all agree to become God's people, and to obey God's commands.

Within a year, the miracle that God had promised happened. Sarah had a baby, a boy called Isaac. Then Abraham and Sarah knew that they were truly blessed by God.

Isaac grew up into a strong boy. Abraham loved him deeply. But one day, something terrible happened. God called Abraham and said,

"Take Isaac up into the hills. I want you to sacrifice him to me."

In those days, people often made sacrifices to God. They used to kill an animal, and burn it as a kind of 'Thank you' prayer. Abraham himself had often done it. But now God was asking him to kill his own son instead!

Abraham remembered that his side of the promise was always to do as God commanded. So he led Isaac out into the hills, giving him a bundle of wood to carry to make the sacrificial fire. The boy did not understand what was happening. Abraham, watching his son, asked himself how he was going to find the strength to do what God wanted.

They came to the hilltop. Abraham built an altar and tied Isaac on top of it. Then he held up a knife, ready to kill his son for God.

Just at that moment, Abraham heard an angel calling to him:

"Abraham stop! Now God knows for certain that you will always obey him. He does not really want you to kill your son! Instead, Isaac shall grow up, and his grandchildren, your descendants, shall found a great nation, just as God promised you."

God kept his promise. For Isaac had 12 grandsons, and they were the founding fathers of Israel, the Jewish people.

UNIT 7
Shabbat Shalom

AIMS

1 The children should know about and be able to describe some of the customs associated with keeping Shabbat.

2 The children should develop their understanding of the religious and family meaning Shabbat holds for Jewish people.

3 The children should explore ways of being caring and responsible in the family.

PREPARATION

For these activities you will need:

● poster 7;

● copies of Activity sheet 7 (page 39) and supplementary activity sheet (page 54).

If possible:

● a loaf of bread (preferably in a plait);

● ingredients for making salt dough (page 54);

● a box or bag of sweet-smelling perfume or spices.

Core activities

1 Special days, special meals
(30 mins)

Talk to the children about their weekly routine. Encourage the children to identify that, e.g. Saturday or Sunday is often different and special. Ask the children to think of reasons why, e.g. few people work; families spend time together and sometimes visit relatives; there are some laws about shops opening on Sundays; some families visit places of worship.

Encourage the children to focus on the idea of a special family meal, asking whether any of the children have a special meal on a given day. Ask them to describe any special foods they eat on this day.

The children can identify other special days associated with special foods, e.g. Id-ul-Fitr, Holi, Christmas, Easter, birthdays etc. Talk about the special events and foods associated with these days.

Ask the children whether they know why, e.g. Sunday is in some way special. Encourage them to identify both that life would be horrible without one day of rest each week, and that Christian religious laws say that you should rest on the seventh day of the week.

2 Shabbat
(15 mins)

Look at poster 7 and use the questions and guidance on the reverse of the poster to draw meaning and information from the picture.

Compare the children's experience with the Jewish experience of Shabbat (e.g. family gathering; special foods; day of rest).

Ensure that the children recognise the importance of Shabbat to Jewish families, the religious reasons for Shabbat, and the rules which govern Shabbat.

3 Quiet day
(45 mins)

Ask the children to imagine a very peaceful day, when nobody worked, nobody rushed around, and people spent time enjoying the company of their family and friends. What would they have to do to ensure that there was peace? Encourage the children to identify, e.g. switching off the phone; not using the car; not having the television on. Ask the children: what would you do without these things?

The children can work in small groups to plan what they would do on this day from 8 a.m. to 8 p.m. During their planned day, there should be peacefulness.

Use Activity sheet 7 (page 39) to help the children to think about how people might feel on such a day. Allocate family roles to each child in the group (father, mother, sister, brother etc.) and ask them to decorate the face to match their character. They should fill in the thought bubble about how this person might feel about the day and what they are going to do.

4 Peace and sweetness
(30 mins)

Remind the children about the importance of the special bread in the celebration of Shabbat. If possible, buy a special loaf, preferably a plaited loaf.

Tell the children that the Jewish word of welcome is 'shalom', which means 'peace'. This greeting is used often during Shabbat.

Share bread by passing it from one to the other. Each child should take a little to eat and say 'shalom' to the child next to them.

When all of the children have tried the bread, pass around a box or bag containing something that smells nice, e.g. perfume or spices.

Everyone can take in the aroma, and whilst they are doing so, ask them to think of a way in which they can make the week ahead a little sweeter for someone.

Shabbat

EXTENSION

Use salt dough to make models of the special plaited bread. A picture of the bread and a recipe for salt dough are given on the supplementary activity sheet on page 54.

Invite a member of the Keep Sunday Special campaign to your school, or find someone who feels strongly about the subject. Arrange a debate with someone who has a different point of view, e.g. someone from a local superstore which opens on a Sunday. If these people are unavailable, you can improvise by allowing children to role-play the campaigner and store manager in a debate. This is a good way to introduce and extend the idea of 'special days', and points raised can be applied more universally to *all* special days.

A more basic approach

The suggestions on this page will help you adapt the Core teaching and learning activities, making them suitable for younger children or those at an earlier stage of development.

1 Special days, special meals

Make some cards with descriptions of activities which might be done on different days of the week, e.g. 'go shopping'; 'go to a place of worship'; 'have a lie-in'; 'go to school'; 'go to work'; 'go to watch a tennis match'; 'go to the doctor'; 'wash the car' and so on. (You can give a simple picture cue for many of the cards.)

Ask the children to sort the cards out into three piles: weekday activities; Saturday activities; Sunday activities. Sit the children in a circle and hold up the cards one at a time. Ask the children to talk about and, preferably, agree on which pile the cards belong to. (The 'go to a place of worship' card can obviously belong to different piles, depending on the children's religion.)

Ask the children to suggest other activities to add to each pile.

Discuss the different kinds of activity in each pile, and the reasons why a day, e.g. Sunday, might be special, e.g. few people work and families spend time together; some families visit a place of worship and so on.

2 Shabbat

The poster activity is suitable for all children.

Ask the children to imagine that they are one of the people in the poster and to draw a large thought bubble in which they can write about the way 'their' person is feeling about the evening ahead and what they are going to talk about with the family.

3 Quiet day

This activity is suitable for all children. Help the children to plan the day by asking them to tell you what are some of their favourite things: favourite games; favourite things to talk about; favourite food; favourite music; favourite books and so on.

These favourite things can be listed, and the children can include them in their plan for the quiet day.

4 Peace and sweetness

Ask the children to make posters which show the word 'peace'. Where appropriate, you can give the word already written for children to decorate with things which remind them of peace.

Listen to some peaceful music, talk about what makes it peaceful, and make a collage of peaceful scenes using pictures from magazines or old calendars.

Special days

What would you do on your special day?
How would you feel?

UNIT 8
Bar and Bat Mitzvah

AIMS

1 The children should know about and be able to describe the ceremonies of Bar Mitzvah and Bat Mitzvah.

2 The children should recognise that such ceremonies play an important part in marking 'stages' of life.

3 The children should develop their understanding of what it means to be responsible for one's own actions.

4 The children should reflect on the qualities they admire in others and aspire to themselves.

PREPARATION

For these activities you will need:

● poster 8;

● copies of Activity sheet 8 (page 43) and supplementary activity sheet (page 55).

Core activities

1 Stages of life
(15 mins)

Where children have already experienced some discussion about the different 'stages' of life, it will be useful to use this activity as a revision exercise. Ask the children to give words which describe a person at each of the 'stages', e.g. 'baby', 'toddler', 'schoolchild'.

Draw a timeline showing different stages of life and write the descriptive words against the ages.

Tell/remind the children that the change from one described stage of life to another is often marked by special occasions, celebrations and ceremonies, e.g. baptism, naming ceremony, wedding.

2 The Bar or Bat Mitzvah ceremony
(30 mins)

Explain to the children that you are going to look at the ways in which Jews celebrate the growing up of their children. Show them poster 8 and use the questions and guidance on the reverse to lead a discussion and draw out meaning from the pictures shown.

3 Whom do I admire?
(30 mins)

The purpose of this activity is to help the children to think about what sort of people they like and admire, and why. It is important for the teacher to help children to understand the distinctions between what a person does, what a person has, and what a person is in terms of character.

Ask the children to think of some adults that they admire and like. They can be family, friends, public or sporting figures. Ask them to write down on Activity sheet

8 (page 43) words or phrases which describe what it is about these people that they particularly like. Is it their lifestyle? Skills? Character?

It might be a good homework activity for some children to find out about their chosen person and complete the activity sheet accordingly. They can also collect photos and cuttings about their person.

As a class, make three lists, headed: what special people do; what special people have; what special people are like. Try to ensure that the third category has plenty of words in it.

4 What I would like to be like

(45 mins)

This activity draws on the lists of words created in the previous activity, about what special people are like.

Remind the children about the Bar/Bat Mitzvah ceremony, in which Jewish boys and girls make a speech during which they say what sort of person they would like to be when they grow up.

Ask the children to choose the word from the list which best describes what sort of person they would like to be when they grow up.

Use the supplementary activity sheet on page 55 for this activity, and ask the children to write their chosen words in the spaces provided.

Finally, ask the children to use their completed supplementary activity sheet to write a short speech as if they were at a Bar or Bat Mitzvah. The speech should include three elements: thanks for presents; thanks to parents for bringing them up; a description of what sort of person they would like to be.

If you feel it is appropriate, the children can be invited to read their speeches to the class.

Bar and Bat Mitzvah

EXTENSION

The children can find out more about famous people whom they admire. The people can be alive today, can be famous in history, or can be famous men or women in the Bible or in Jewish history.

The children can make notes about the people they choose under three headings: what special people do; what special people have; what special people are like.

Ask the children whether they notice anything which the people they have found out about have in common.

A more basic approach

The suggestions on this page will help you adapt the Core teaching and learning activities, making them suitable for younger children or those at an earlier stage of development.

1 Stages of life

Give the children cards with words which describe a person at each of the stages, e.g. 'baby', 'toddler', 'schoolchild'.

Ask them to put the words in order. Ask them to guess the age when the change from one stage to another takes place.

Use the words to make a timeline.

Give the children another set of cards, this time with the names of ceremonies which mark times of change, e.g. baptism, wedding.

Ask the children to put the cards on the right place on the timeline.

2 The Bar or Bat Mitzvah ceremony

The poster activity is suitable for all children. If you have any Jewish artefacts, such as a scroll and a prayer shawl, use them to demonstrate what the boy or girl would do in the synagogue.

Concentrate on talking about how the boy and girl must feel, to stand up in front of lots of people and read or make a speech.

How do the children feel about reading or speaking aloud to people?

3 Whom do I admire?

Choose one famous person, and find a picture of that person.

Tell the children about the person.

Prepare some cards with words which describe the person. As in the Core activity, the descriptions should fall under the following three headings: what the person does; what the person has; what the person is like.

Ask the children to sort the words into the three lists.

4 What I would like to be like

Take the words which you and the children agreed, in the last activity, should be placed under the 'what the person is like' heading.

Talk to the children about other special words which could be added to the list.

Give the children a piece of paper with the words 'When I grow up I want to be . . .' written at the top. Ask the children to pick out the words from the list, and write them underneath in order of importance.

The children can copy their words, or write with guidance. Encourage them to talk about the order that they have chosen and why.

If appropriate, the children can practise reading their lists and read them to the class.

ACTIVITY SHEET 8   **Whom do I admire?**

Draw the person you admire the most and write why you admire them.

_____

_____

_____

_____

_____

UNIT 9
A Jewish wedding

AIMS

1 The children should know about and be able to describe wedding customs in Judaism.

2 The children should develop their understanding of the way in which relationships are built from both sides.

PREPARATION

For these activities you will need:

- poster 9;
- copies of Activity sheet 9 (page 47) and supplementary activity sheet (page 56);
- paper cups and juice.

If possible:

- a Jewish visitor or a video of a Jewish wedding;
- a video camera;
- a sheet/large piece of material/large sheet of paper;
- poles and other materials to make a chuppah.

Core activities

1 Under the chuppah
(15 mins)

Show the children poster 9. Use the questions and guidance on the reverse of the poster as the basis of a discussion about marriage and Jewish weddings.

If possible, invite a Jewish visitor into your class. Ask them to talk about their wedding or show a video of a Jewish wedding.

2 The wedding contract
(15 mins)

Use Activity sheet 9 (page 47). It shows a jigsaw pattern.

Divide the children into small groups. If possible, there should be both boys and girls in each group. Ask each group to discuss, agree on and draw up a contract. They should decide seven things which partners should promise each other in order to show how much they care for each other.

Ask the children to think about whether any might be more relevant to girls or to boys.

3 Seven blessings
(30 mins)

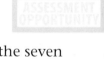

Remind the children about the seven blessings in the Jewish wedding ceremony. Ask the children to draw a line or a bouquet of seven flowers. Ask them to think about what good wishes or blessings they would wish for people who were getting married. Ask the children to write one wish or blessing on each flower.

Colour the flowers, and use them to decorate a display area, window or door panel as a blessings garden.

4 A wedding album
(30 mins)

Use the supplementary activity sheet on page 56 for this activity. On this sheet, there are simple descriptions of the six stages of the wedding in one set of balloons, and the symbolic meaning in another six balloons.

The children should arrange the statements into the correct order, and match the correct description to the correct symbolic meaning.

Use the six description bubbles as a basis for drawing a wedding album. Organise children into groups of six. Give each child the responsibility of drawing a picture of one of the six stages.

Make the six pictures into a short album.

5 Mazel tov! (Good luck!)
(30 mins)

Remind the children that the final stage of a Jewish marriage is where the groom crushes the glass under his foot, and the congregation shout 'Mazel tov!'

Ask the children to think about the good luck they might like to wish other people in the class or other people elsewhere.

Ask them to write down some of the things they would want to say.

Sit the class in a circle. Give everyone a paper cup and a little juice to represent wine. Ask each person who has a good-luck wish to read it out. All the children should shout out 'Mazel tov!' together, drink the 'wine', and crush the paper cups under their feet after they have spoken.

A Jewish wedding

EXTENSION

Make a large model of a chuppah. Decorate the poles with tinsel.

The children can prepare a series of scenes or tableaux, each one based on one of the six stages in the Jewish wedding ceremony.

Let the children demonstrate the marriage ceremony, showing each stage. Some children can use the words on the supplementary activity sheet on page 56 to add a commentary, explaining the significance of each stage of the wedding.

A more basic approach

The suggestions on this page will help you adapt the Core teaching and learning activities, making them suitable for younger children or those at an earlier stage of development.

1 Under the chuppah

The poster activity is suitable for all children.

Use the information on the supplementary activity sheet (page 56) to prepare cards with simple drawings/pictures cues and simple wording which 'describes' the six events in the wedding. Show each card in turn to establish the order of events.

2 The wedding contract

Use the idea on Activity sheet 9 (page 47), but prepare only four pieces of jigsaw. The children will have to think of fewer promises.

You may need to write out whatever the children say.

Prepare a sheet or blanket to represent the chuppah. Coach the children to read their promises, and ask them to read or say them standing under the sheet.

3 Seven blessings

Remind the children about the seven blessings, as in the Core activity.

Give each of the children a petal from the large flower shapes, and help them to think of a suitable blessing. Write it on their petal.

The children can colour the flowers and use them to decorate a display area.

4 A wedding album

Use the cards you made for the first 'more basic' activity, 'Under the chuppah'.

Ask the children to mime or demonstrate the six activities which are included in the Jewish wedding.

If the children become sufficiently adept, video the scene and play it back to the class, or in an assembly.

5 Mazel tov! (Good luck!)

Remind the children of the time, during the wedding ceremony, when the congregation shout 'Mazel tov!'

The Core activity is suitable for all children. The children can practise saying 'Mazel tov!' in unison. Some children may have difficulties writing down their blessings, but will be able to write with guidance/copy their words, or, if appropriate, can tell them to the teacher to write down.

ACTIVITY SHEET 9   The wedding-contract jigsaw

Can you think of seven things partners should promise?
Write the words.

UNIT 10
Heaven and Earth

AIMS

1 The children should be able to experience and respond to an amazing picture.

2 The children should be able to recognise that such experiences are interpreted in different ways by different people.

3 The children should encounter a psalm as an example of someone's response to an experience.

PREPARATION

For these activities you will need:

- poster 10;

- copies of Activity sheet 10 (page 51);

- a Bible;

- music to create atmosphere, e.g. *Planets Suite* by Holst/the soundtrack for the film *Apollo 13*.

Core activities

1 The Earth is . . .
(30 mins)

Pin the poster to a wall or board, with plenty of space around it where children can pin pieces of paper. Cover the poster, so that the picture can be revealed when you are ready. Arrange the class so that they can all see the poster, and have pencil and paper ready to write. Ensure that the class are calm, relaxed and quiet.

Explain to the children that you are going to show them a poster and play them some music. You do not want them to say anything, or respond in any way at first: they should just look at the poster, listen to the music and think about how the picture makes them feel.

Show the poster and play the music. Appropriate music for this activity would be, e.g. *Planets Suite* by Holst; the *Apollo 13* film soundtrack; *Chariots of Fire* film soundtrack; the opening from *2001, A Space Odyssey* (film).

After a few minutes, ask each child to write down one word which they feel best describes the picture of the Earth or their response to it. When all of the children have written their word, ask them to take their words and pin them around the poster to create a display.

Use the questions and guidance on the reverse of the poster to draw meaning from the picture.

2 The moon and stars
(30 mins)

Tell the children a brief version of the story of King David, as described on the reverse of the poster.

Ask the children to imagine how David, the shepherd, must have felt as he sat on the high hillside, with an immense vista all around him, gazing up at the stars in the night sky. The children can draw upon their own experiences of looking at the night sky. Encourage the children to give answers expressing particularly a sense of awe, wonder and peace. They should consider how they felt about themselves in relation to the hugeness of the night sky.

Read Psalm 8 to the class, at least twice, so that they can begin to understand it. If possible, show it on an OHP or write it out on large paper so that the class can read it.

Talk about the use of language and briefly summarize the meaning of the psalm as

'When I look at Creation, I realise how small humans are, and praise you for making humans special and the highest form of Creation.'

The children can compare the feelings and experience of David, as expressed in the psalm, with their own experiences, looking at the stars and looking at the poster.

3 Creation poems
(45 mins)

Remind the children of their responses to the poster and the music, and the response of David to the moon and stars.

Set the children the task of writing a poem about the poster. They can use the words pinned around the poster in Activity 1 in their poem. The children can use Activity sheet 10 (page 51) to record their poems.

When they have finished writing their poem, the children can decorate their page. Collect the poems together and bind them into a class book of poems.

4 All Creation, great and small
(15 mins)

Read the story of the Creation from Genesis I to the children.

You can explain to the children that the writer would have been a person who was 'inspired' to write, both by his beliefs and by 'Creation' (or the world as he saw it). Try to develop the children's understanding that this story is not an account of events in a real or factual sense, but that the writer would have felt that what he was trying to say about his God was better told as a story. He wanted people to 'dig out' from the story the idea of the mystery of Creation.

The Earth from space

EXTENSION

Ask a group of children to each learn a line of Psalm 8. Let the group rehearse speaking the psalm with meaning.

Let the group speak the psalm to the whole class or in an assembly.

Ask the children to find out more about the story of King David.

If you can, secure a copy of the video of *Apollo 13* and show the children edited highlights of two moments in the film: when the central character (an astronaut) looks into the night sky from Earth, and places his thumb in the air to cover the moon; and when he looks at the Earth from space, and is able to cover it with his thumb. Use these as the basis for a class discussion, e.g. about the music that accompanies each extract and how it makes the children feel (or seems to be trying to get them to feel) about what they are seeing.

49

A more basic approach

The suggestions on this page will help you adapt the Core teaching and learning activities, making them suitable for younger children or those at an earlier stage of development.

1 The Earth is . . .

This activity is suitable for all children. Those children who find writing difficult can be encouraged to choose their words and write them with guidance, or you can write them out where appropriate.

2 The moon and stars

The story, and discussion about the story, is suitable for many children, and they will be able to respond to questions at their own level. Talking about David's feelings and sense of wonder will, equally, be differentiated by response.

The whole of David's psalm is likely to be difficult for the children to understand. Read the psalm to the children with expression, and go on to pick out important words from verses three and four, to concentrate on in discussion.

Coach the children to be able to read or repeat the lines, and let them speak them. Encourage them to speak them with feeling, as if they were David on the dark hillside or an astronaut in a spaceship.

3 Creation poems

Give the children the following words: 'Earth', 'sun', 'moon', 'stars', 'planets', written out on card/displayed.

Take each one of these words in turn, and ask the children to choose another word to go with it. They should choose a word from those that were placed around the poster in the first activity. The word they choose should describe their feelings about the Earth, etc.

Ask the children to make up a sentence which includes both words, e.g., 'Earth' and 'splendid', as in 'The Earth is a splendid place'.

If they cannot write their own sentence, copy it down for them.

Repeat this process with each word, until the child has five sentences. They can then be encouraged to think about how to arrange the sentences into a poem.

4 All Creation, great and small

This activity is suitable for all children. Ensure that you choose a simple version of the story so that children can understand.

ACTIVITY SHEET 10   **My Creation poem**

Choose the best words from those pinned around the
poster. Use the words to help you write a poem about space.
Make sure you also use all of these words in your poem:

space   Earth   star

sun   moon   planet

Being sorry and beginning again

Look up these words in your dictionary and write down what they mean.

Repentance _____

Atonement _____

Forgiveness _____

Make and complete the following chart.

Making resolutions

	I will try to:	what will make this hard:	what will make this easier:
for myself:			
for my parents:			
for my friends:			
for my school:			
for the world:			

The salt dough made from this recipe can be kept for many weeks in a polythene bag in a fridge.

You need:

  2 cups plain flour

  1 cup salt

  2 cups water

  2 tablespoons cooking oil

  2 teaspoons cream of tartar

What to do:

1 Put all the ingredients into a pan.

2 Cook over a medium heat, stirring continuously. (The mixture will probably go lumpy at first, but carry on cooking!)

3 The mixture will bind together and come away from the sides of the pan quite quickly. Turn out onto a table and knead. (You will not need to put flour on the table.)

4 Bake the dough for two hours in a medium oven, or until baked hard.

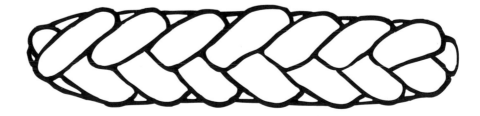

UNIT 8 SUPPLEMENTARY ACTIVITY SHEET

I would like to be . . .

1 Write your chosen word in the space.

When I grow up, I would like to be:

____

2 Write your Bar/Bat Mitzvah speech. Think carefully about your answers.

How will you thank everybody for all of your presents?

____

____

____

How will you thank your parents for bringing you up?

____

____

What would you like to be like when you grow up?

____

____

3 Draw a picture to show how you will look.

The rabbi blesses the couple . . .

The rabbi reads the ketubah, the marriage agreement . . .

The bride joins the groom under the chuppah . . .

They drink wine from the same cup . . .

The groom crushes a wine glass on the floor . . .

The groom places a ring on the bride's finger . . .

which represents the couple's future home.

to remind them there will be bad times as well as good.

so that God will bless them.

to show they will share a life together.

to show that the groom has promised to take care of his wife.

to show that she is now his wife.